The Half Inflated Beach Ball Full of My Whispers

The Half Inflated Beach Ball Full of My Whispers

Nicely Typed Up In This Book

Blythe Lochlan

Blythe Lochlan
2014

First Printing: 2013

ISBN: 978-1-291-64440-1

Acknowledgements

Thanks to,

My limited circle of friends and those who have pushed me forward, the nice lady in the coffee shop, those idiots around me and mainly my past lovers whose antics broke my heart into some of these little pieces of writing.

.The Light Within.

Predictably those
shadows creep over again
flawlessly stitched together
by expert craftsmen.

Locked together
black branched fingers overhead
form skeletal rafters
a thick caged chamber.

I take from my heart a beeswax candle,
lantern shape sculpted
that you installed.

With lightsaber strokes I part
my shrinking coffin.
Life behind these bars
cold to my delicate touch
sane thoughts buried
deep away
on limping crutch
your candle begins to falter.

I know you cannot warm me forever.
Alone with gritted teeth
I pull at these glass sharp branches
laboured hands soon bleed
through gloom decapitating snatches.
I build a fire
from these memories
and light it with your love.

It soon burns
with a growing thirst
warming me, through expelled gloom
I have have the room to breathe.

Tearing down a ruined childhood
to feed this hunger
a gurn breaks out on my wincing face,
awkward, soon settles
like a content cat
into a relaxed smile
below my soot smudged nose.

This woodland, now green and open
the leaves soft under scabbed dirty palms
I blow out this candle and return it to my heart.

.The Result Of Active Cuddles.

Rain reflects
our naked form
in prisms of rainbow shades.
That sweet sex smell.
Dissipates
on cold breeze
from slung open window.
Carried through
into the other rooms
in which we fuck.
We lay panting and satisfied
as the breeze
shaves us naked of our
tingly sweat.

.Giants Map.

The contour lines
on this browning pleated map
are the recorded results of
unkempt emotions
left to run over this
boundryless sullen body.
Leaving behind circling tracks around
excavated areas of
self inflicted rage.

Those calligraphy cut markings
that those "experts" from all over
come to study,
yet no one,
not even those most loved and trusted
could give a definition
nor explanation to the origin.

Your world where you live
and this giant looking
through tear filled eyes,
reflecting back all those
soul searching looks from strangers.

This punishment was received on a different plane,
in a different age,
where now forgiveness would cradle.

But here those received wounds
do not hurt
a snapshot of stagnation,

evidence carved into his chest
for future generations to see.
A warning
the giants keep of the grass sign to all.

Nothing hurts until the following sunrise
where heading towards the shower
the automaton giant creaks and stretches
a wooded seat taking his own
burdening inner weight.
He humps himself into the white lined
sterile cubicle.
Red eyes and staring
focusing, blinking in morse code
at the shower dial with
the suspicion of Dave
towards Hall in 2001:Space Odyssey.

Turning the dial to allow
water to heat and steam
to cleanse whisky blocked pores.
Captured screams echo at first contact
of heated water
as scalded blisters already under taught skin
boil into venom,
injected violently
into the giants
bloodstream creating maximum destruction.

Crawling back on wasted limbs,
the safety of under his bed
to recover
his low fort
where no one would look for a giant.

Calendar falling into autumn leaves
as this
forgotten stone face cracks,
cold to anyone’s touch.

Yet waits
like a forgotten book
to have the dust
blown from his emotion starved face
by your lips
for gentle fingers to
run over delicate features.

Slow blinkered eyes focus
into the stare of a homesick sailor
looking for home,
looking for what he hopes is there
rather than look at what is here.
The bastard coward.

Bass noted voice
drawn through lips that need retuning,
lies are spoken
his truth caught on a catapult
hurled further back down inside
where they burn and power
the giants anger.

That constant burning indigestion
forces the giant
to clutch his belly and hurl himself
in cramp to the floor.

He calls for his steed to carry him in
drink to the other plane

where he can recover from these mortal wounds.

In time scars heal and fade
as ink spots on turned notepad pages
these pages are filled,
read and read further on
until those scars are nothing more than fullstops.

This giant stands too tall
for people to see the imperfections.

This giant is me.

.Haikus.

Lunch time extended
building emptied quickly.
Thank you fire drill.

Waitress leans over
table wiped, jiggling view.
Remember to tip.

Pointy chin feature
sex position, hold on tight!
Called the cliff hanger.

Clouds race across sky
fat cumulus soon chased down.
Sprinty cirrus wins.

Waiter's pants too tight
thrusts at menu selection.
Special of the day.

Lonely bean in tin
did not follow my orders.
Dead comrades on toast.

Thick condensation
sticks to windows, exhaled breaths.
Our satisfied dreams.

Self broken fingers
bones twisted to release pain.
No defensive fist.

Durping at his desk
wooden dipping bird movement.
Bored office worker.

Shuddering bus seat
large cobbled road works detour.
Surprise orgasm.

Hard finger fucking
from touchscreen Iphone users.
Satisfied girlfriends.

.Heart Shaped Scar.

I miss the way
you nibbled at me
like a corn on the cob
with pro typewriting pace
greedily.
Brings a soft smile
to my hard face
the one so lucky.

Days drawn short
a continuous winter
now only my coat warms me
with face buried under a frown
reluctantly.
Again this free fall
begin to drown
just one gesture.

In the shower
I still rub that scar
now completely healed
from when we rolled
down that field
we tumbled so far
in each other's arms.
Picnic basket fondue
surrounded by crops
and collapsed barns.

The only reminder
I have of you.
I can't get rid of it
except to hide you under a larger scar.

.Back Of The Sofa.

Fumbling on your parents' sofa, super keen
oh what it was, to be an excitable teen
unbuttoning clothes with trembling fingers
every bit of new flesh in my mind it lingers.

Bra unclasped, that's second base conquered
time to head for third as I move southward
my sweaty hand is on the inside of her knee
no complaints yet, carry on we both agree.

Trembling, I swallow, my hand trundles on
slipping about, her legs? Are coated in Teflon?
Like an old freight train through the night
unstoppable with its lusty teenage might.

Beads of exasperated sweat form on my head
like that itchy bomb disposable expert Fred,
my fingers gingerly frolic about blind,
with my inexperience she doesn't mind.

At last! Fingertips press against something,
plural something's, that seem to be jingling?!?!
Frozen pause, tentative fingers touch,
What's this? It all seems a bit too much.

Seem to find more, pulling my hand down
found some coins, and a pen leads to a frown
More wild tongue snogging and some digging
Yields only a 9 volt battery, rusting.

Reaching further, what more will I retrieve?
Turned off, she ups and asks me to leave
confused and freaked out, left in a trauma,
I had my hand down the back of the sofa.

.Your Kiss.

I would have to kiss every girl
in the world
to find the one
that kisses like you.

Fascinated by your every move
I would watch you silently.

Forgotten your face,
your touch all I have left
is the fading memory of your soft lips.

Scared I would crush you
under all this dead weight
You could warm me
from twenty paces
any closer and I burn.

.Take Hold.

Take hold,
we're bracing for impact
this time is ours
and is fading fast.
Full of the arrogance told
ignoring the few who are true
that self placed status.
Growing downfall.

Drown them,
with their own silence
so you won't hear
the alarms calling.
To arms, seen as traitors
replaced social wannabe uniform
with that of a soldier.
Rise up together.

Defend,
the enemy you seek out
is your own self
Traitor of this race.
Dragged down by no morals
no backbone to carry this world
like all the king's men.
We all fall down.

.Tanka.

Letterbox circles
student below awaits results.
taught by his mistress.
Brown envelope falls
Red rose inside, A+

.My List.

Everyday I order a cup of tea
from the pretty waitress.
Just to watch you bring it over
to see your polite smile.
To share that brief moment
of intimacy with you.

On the palm of my hand
in permanent marker.
I will write a to-do list
for each and every day.
On it will command,
a cuddle,
a kiss - underlined twice.
A back rub,
to do the washing up,
to fetch chips in the rain.
I will tick these off daily
for as long as I am with you.

.The Letterbox Pervert.

The letterbox pervert
follows dog walkers home.
He waits 'til nightfall
then strikes,
smearing his willy in dog food
and poking it through
the letterbox and whistles
to get the dog's attention.
"Good boy" he squirms against the door.

.Haikus.

Your breath inflates soul
Fingers cover patchwork holes.
Full of your warm love.

I want repeat ski jumps
slalom down your perfect nose
Soft cleavage landing.

This hubcap vessel
beaten as I soothe harsh waves.
Your ocean of love.

Wise old man once said.
"You can't make a cup of tea,
without a teabag."

"Stand still, yes like that"
draws around with black marker.
My keepsake of you.

.Should Of Said.

Bothered still by things I should of said
continue to haunt me until the day I'm dead
Never stood up against father's beatings,
still even now someone touching me stings.

Should of told my mother how useless
she was questions answered with "because because",
from her delivered shouting's, saying go away
I am still silent and hidden to this very day.

I struggled with every moment you came near
not knowing what to do full of panicking fear.
All I ever wanted to do is show you with a kiss
how I felt, never did and it's now what I miss.

Reaching out my hand trembling scared
to hold you and to whisper what I've prepared,
instead I was silent and my love I did betray.
Gained my voice, by then it was too late to say.

Here in this jail, scared, waiting to be found
still nothing, like a dusty piano with no sound.
They say that a man without family is no-one
without you I'm alone, it cannot be undone.

.My Grans Death.

How my mother broke the news
that my gran was dead.
She shouted up the stairs to me,
as I read, sat on my bed.

.Follow On.

Our mothers sleep with casual strangers
separated father's teary eyed, drink alone.
Both unaware of the dangers
that we face down this
darken road.
Journey starts, can no longer postpone.

Divided here we have collapsed, fallen
neighbours replaced with people unknown.
Society completely stolen
by our own automation
shutting down.
A new future for us needs to be shown.

Streetlights pulse like a weak heartbeat
lighting only just a few steps further ahead.
These strangers we meet
to combine our touch feeling our way.
This path found with our fingers outspread.

.Sweater Than A Stolen Square.

You taste sweeter than
a stolen square of chocolate,
this shock and awe assault
on my taste buds.
Leaves my senses disorientated
you're that dessert
I can never finish.
Full after feasting on your beauty,
this burning indigestion
keeps me warm
I will take the rest home
in a doggy bag
for when I'm ready for it.

.Haikus.

Sharp caws for order
crows take organised council.
On knotted branched seats.

Fat man's black t-shirt
sweating stretched salt sundial rings.
Afternoon wilts on.

Baby in push chair
gives mother quizzical frown.
Pushed over cobbles.

Lots of snow angels
litter outside local pubs.
Coincidence?

My Roxy hotel
where I come to weather storms.
Deep within your heart.

Fumbling in the dark
trying to unclasp her bra.
Gah!! That's my watch strap!

Sunburnt skin peeling
shirt donated for a sail.
I will get to you.

Pokémon trainers
never bathe with Pikachu.
Electrocution.

Lit Chinese dragon
formed from taxi headlights, snakes.
Crawling down highstreet.

Tipsy suggestions
whispered into partners ears.
Deny when sober.

Anticipation,
private burlesque show for me.
Ejaculation.

Lay waiting on grass,
for you. Walk into my life.
Hope you wear a skirt.

Lusty gaze at breasts
captured on facebook for all. A
waits girlfriend's wrath.

To restart my heart
resuscitation only.
Requires your touch.

Pretty hole punched eyes
lighting this darkness inside.
Warm glow on my heart.

Snogging sweatily,
her glitter make-up transferred.
Look like crap tranny.

Bite hard at my soul
Feast on my deep misery.
Your lips blue then black.

Lonely shy woman,
to get her sexual kicks.
Uses spin cycle.

Tobacco pouch sniffed
pressed hard against lonely lips.
Your kiss sorely missed.

Bed sheet contour lines
map last night's expedition.
On the floor we wake.

www.ingramcontent.com/pod-product-compliance
Ingram Content Group UK Ltd.
Pitfield, Milton Keynes, MK11 3LW, UK
UKHW020227250726
13967UKWH00001B/237